Contents

All Kinds of Transport

Are you ready to travel around the world and learn about the transport used by children just like you? You'll find out how people get across deserts and over mountains, through cities and along rivers. You'll see all sorts of transport, from trains and aeroplanes to boats and horse-drawn carts.

Planes aren't the only form of air transport. What do you think makes this American hot air balloon rise into the sky? Find out on page 23.

Boats allow us to travel across lakes and rivers. What do you think this Peruvian girl's boat is made from? Find out the answer on page 8.

In cold countries, skiing is a quick way to move across the snow. Learn why this Norwegian boy is skiing with poles on page 11.

Animals are still used for transport in many countries. Discover why horses are so important to these Mongolian boys on page 20.

Some forms of transport are works of art! Why do you think these Malaysian trishaws are decorated with flowers? Find out why on page 27.

Take a journey around the world to discover the transport used by children just like you!

Cross a City

Every day, around 150,000 cars, trucks, buses and bicycles drive around the Indian city of Delhi. It's a noisy squeeze for everyone, especially as they have to share the roads with much older and slower types of transport, such as this cart pulled by an ox.

This ox cart is delivering sacks of grain around Delhi. It's giving lifts to people, too.

Taxis of all kinds criss-cross the world's cities. The taxis in New York have been painted yellow for over a hundred years, so that people can easily recognise them and hail them in the street.

Official taxi cabs in New York have to be painted yellow by law.

This young New Yorker is hailing a city taxi, in a gesture used all over the world. She is putting her arm out to signal to the taxi driver to stop.

The three cable car routes in La Paz are coloured red, green and yellow – the colours of the Bolivian flag. This is the red line.

You can take a record-breaking cable car to avoid the traffic in the Bolivian city of La Paz. The city's cable cars are the highest in the world, at around 3962m above sea level. Stretching for 9.65km across the city, the cable car system in La Paz is also the longest in the world.

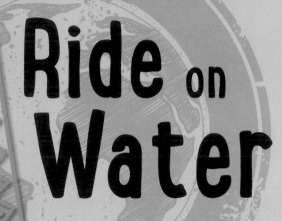

Ride on Water

This Vietnamese family are on the Hâu River. There are lots of villages along the riverbanks, and boating is the easiest way to travel from place to place. The family might be going to a local floating market, where they will buy food from stalls on boats.

Sometimes there are heavy monsoon rains in Vietnam, so this boat has a covering in case the weather is wet.

This girl's unusual boat is called a balsa de totora. It is being used on Lake Titicaca, which is between Peru and Bolivia in South America. The boat is made from the reeds that grow around the lake. Boats have been made in this way for thousands of years.

This girl lives on an island on Lake Titicaca in South America. She needs a boat to get around the lake.

Fishermen who work on Lake Titicaca use small one-person canoes called caballitos, made from reeds.

These Sri Lankan boys power and steer their boat by paddling it.

These boys are paddling their hollowed-out log canoe on the Maduganga River in Sri Lanka. Their home is in a swampy wetland area, with lots of streams and ponds. It is hard to build roads across the boggy ground, so the best way to get around is by boat.

Through the Snow

Dukha children spend their days travelling around with their family, herding their reindeer.

In very cold places, people need special transport that can get through the snow. The Dukha tribe, who live in northern Mongolia, use reindeer to travel across the snowy countryside. They look after herds of reindeer, and they choose the strongest ones to ride.

Snowmobiles are great for getting around in wintery conditions. Snowmobiles have tracks instead of wheels, so they don't need a road to run on and they don't get stuck in deep snow. Snowmobiles have motorbike-style engines to power them, and they can carry one or two people onboard.

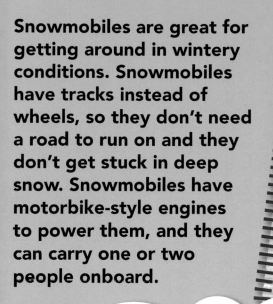

Skis fitted at the front of a snowmobile help it to slide over snow. The skis are curved upwards so they don't stick into snowdrifts.

When a car can't get through the snow, skiing or snowboarding is sometimes the easiest way to travel around. In snowy countries, everybody learns to ski from an early age. There are two types of skiing – fast downhill skiing and cross-country skiing, where skiers stride over snow on thin skis.

This Norwegian boy is cross-country skiing. The poles help him to balance and push himself forwards through the snow.

Take to the Tracks

This bullet train is zooming past Mount Fuji in Japan.

The world's fastest train system, the shinkansen, runs across Japan, carrying over 150 million passengers a year. The trains are nicknamed bullet trains because they are so fast, speeding through the countryside at up to 320kph. The record for the fastest train of all goes to the Japanese-designed Maglev train, which can travel at over 600kph.

Maglev trains use electric-powered magnets to hover above the track. This Maglev train connects Shanghai city centre to the airport.

This crowded Cambodian bamboo train is called a nori. It is a platform of bamboo slats fitted with a small engine, which travels along the railway tracks at about 15kph. If another bamboo train comes the other way, the train with the fewest passengers onboard is lifted off the track to let the other one pass.

Bamboo railways ferry people between villages in the area of Batambang, Cambodia.

The Children's Railway in Kiev, Ukraine, is run by children. All summer long they help out as the drivers, conductors and train engineers. There were once many Children's Railways of this kind, built to give schoolchildren the chance to train for jobs.

Some of the children that run the Children's Railway in Kiev will go on to work on the railways when they leave school.

Explore a Desert

These quad bikers are about to take a ride through the world's biggest desert, the Sahara in North Africa. A quad bike is a good option for driving on soft sand because its four big wheels spread out its weight, helping to prevent it from sinking and getting stuck.

Sand can sting when it hits your skin, so these quad bikers have covered their faces with scarves.

This boy and his dad are riding in an off-road dune buggy in Baja, California, USA. Dune buggies are raced across the coastal sands in this area. They have big, wide tyres and an engine at the back that helps to weigh down the lightweight buggy as it zips over the dunes.

Dune buggies don't have any windows, so this boy is protecting his face with goggles.

When this Ethiopian girl wants to change the direction that her camel is moving in, she pulls on the string wrapped around her camel's head.

For centuries, people have travelled across Middle Eastern and African deserts by camel. This girl lives in the deserts of Ethiopia. Her camel is the ideal transport around her dusty, sandy home. It has wide padded feet to stop it from sinking into the soft sand, and a woolly coat that keeps it cool in hot weather and warm on chilly nights.

Camels have three eyelids and two sets of eyelashes to help protect their eyes from sand.

Up a Mountain

It's tough work carrying things up mountains, but donkeys are experts. They are strong and good at keeping their footing on loose, rocky paths. This donkey is carrying its load up the world's highest mountain range, the Himalayas. There are no roads here for trucks to drive on, so donkeys are an important form of transport.

This Himalayan donkey has bells attached to his harness. If it falls behind, or goes up too far ahead on the mountain path, its owner will be able to hear where it is.

Mountain bikes are good for riding on bumpy off-road tracks, such as this one in the USA.

Today, mountain bikes are popular everywhere, but when they were invented in California in the late 1970s, some people said they would never catch on! They have a strong frame and tough tyres, which are perfect for cycling down rocky paths. Experienced mountain bikers can ride down steep mountain paths, with jumps and sharp turns.

This summertime chairlift is on Mount Balo in the Italian Alps. You can see Lake Garda in the distance.

This wintertime chairlift is on the ski slopes of Colorado, USA.

Chairlifts travel up and down mountainsides on cables. They can give passengers a fantastic countryside view in summer and take them to hard-to-reach ski slopes in winter. They were invented in the USA in the 1930s, when skiing holidays were beginning to become popular.

Festival Transport

In Venice's historic boat parade, the rowers dress in uniforms once worn by the servants of rich Venetian nobles.

Every September, the canals of Venice, Italy, fill with a parade of historic boats, called the Regata Storica. Crowds line the waterways to see the impressive gondolas (Venetian rowing boats) and barges. The festival dates back around 500 years, to a time when Venice's wealthy rulers were rowed around town to show off their wealth and power.

Carnival floats like these often help to raise money for charity. People watching the parade throw money onto the floats if they like the design.

Parades are held around the world at festival times, and trucks are sometimes transformed into incredible decorated floats for these events. These floats are from the Viareggio Carnival, which is held in Italy every February at the start of the Christian festival of Lent. The floats are driven through the town as part of a parade.

Elephants provide the transport at the Buat Chang celebration. This parade takes place in the Sukhothai region of Thailand, where boys aged 10 and above are ordained (accepted in a special ceremony) to train as Buddhist monks. The new monks dress up and ride on elephants in a procession.

In the Thai Buat Chang parade, the elephants are painted with colourful patterns and decorated with ribbons.

All Kinds of Horses

Horses have been used as transport for thousands of years. In Mongolia, where these children live, they are still very important. Nearly every family has horses for riding and to help with carrying things. Female horses are kept for their milk, which is made into the popular Mongolian drink, kumis.

Horses are so important in Mongolia that there is a famous saying: 'a Mongolian without a horse is like a bird without wings'.

These well-dressed children are riding an Andalucian horse at the Feria de Abril in Sevilla, Spain. Andalucian horses are prized for their beauty and intelligence. At the springtime fair, horse-drawn carriages and riders parade through the city, with their finest Andalucian horses on display.

Many horse riders dress in traditional Spanish clothing at the Feria de Abril in Sevilla.

This Mexican Mennonite family have used modern rubber tyres and plastic poles to make a traditional horse-drawn buggy.

These children are from the Mennonite community in Yucatan, Mexico. Mennonite people have religious beliefs that do not allow them to use modern transport. They ride everywhere in horse-drawn buggies, never using a car.

Take to the Air

Seaplanes are especially useful for reaching lakes and rivers in areas without any roads. They can land directly on water or ice, and are fitted with ski-style floats, which keep them from sinking in the water.

These seaplanes are used by people who commute to work from Victoria to Vancouver in Canada.

Seaplane pilots need to be skilful at landing on water. This seaplane is landing on a US lake.

This boy is flying over Long Beach in California, USA. He is not in an aeroplane, though. He is in a blimp, which is like a giant balloon full of gas. He is riding with the pilot in a passenger car called a gondola beneath the gas-filled section of the blimp.

Gas keeps this blimp up in the air but it has an engine, propellers and a tail controlled by the pilot to steer it.

Look closely and you will see people riding in a basket under this hot air balloon in New Mexico, USA. It floats because it is filled with hot air that is heated by a burner beneath the balloon. Hot air is lighter than cool air, so it rises, taking the balloon with it.

The balloon pilot controls the burner to heat or cool the air in the balloon, making it rise or sink.

Win a Race

These children are competing in a soapbox derby in Kiel, Germany. Soapbox derby racing cars were once made out of large wooden crates used to store soap, which is how they got their name. In a soapbox derby, the homemade mini cars speed down a slope, with only gravity moving them along.

Soapbox derby cars are made at home using recycled equipment such as baby-buggy wheels.

36

Lots of children make themed soapbox derby cars, such as this horse car.

Go-karts come in different shapes and sizes. These go-karts have room for one person, but some are two-seater.

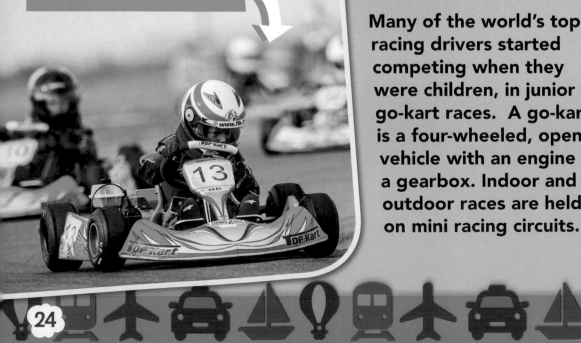

13

Many of the world's top racing drivers started competing when they were children, in junior go-kart races. A go-kart is a four-wheeled, open vehicle with an engine and a gearbox. Indoor and outdoor races are held on mini racing circuits.

BMX races are fast and furious contests between bicycle riders on a purpose-built track with lumps and bumps to cross. Races take less than a minute but they are packed with action. These young riders are competing at a BMX competition in Verona, Italy.

A BMX bicycle has 50-cm wheels. Its light but strong frame makes it ideal for fast racing over bumpy ground.

Decorated Transport

This 'camioneta' bus carries passengers around Guatemala in Central America. Visitors to the country sometimes call this type of bus a 'chicken bus' because local people are often seen carrying their chickens onboard. This bus started out as a school bus in the USA or Canada, but once it got to Guatemala, it got some colourful new decorations.

Each Guatemalan camioneta bus is decorated differently, and their drivers are very proud of them. They are works of art on wheels!

In Pakistan, truck drivers customise their trucks with paint, mirrors, tassels and large carved wooden sections bolted on to the truck body. These vehicles are called 'jingle trucks' because they often have dangling chimes that jingle as the truck drives along.

Pakistani truck drivers spend lots of money trying to make their trucks look impressive, adding lots of extra decoration.

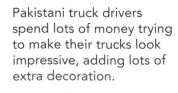

26

These children are riding in a bicycle taxi called a trishaw through the streets of Malacca in Malaysia. The trishaw is decorated with flowers to make it eye-catching for customers, who sit alongside the driver under the umbrella. Every trishaw in town is decorated differently.

The decorated trishaws in Malacca are a popular tourist attraction.

Amazing Transport

This man is on a vintage bicycle called a penny-farthing. It was a popular type of cycle in the late 1800s, before the typical bicycle shape we use today was invented. It's not surprising that penny-farthing riders often injured themselves falling off!

This penny-farthing rider is showing off his vintage machine in Brisbane, Australia.

This car is a 'weinermobile', one of the most famous unusual vehicles in the USA. It has been customised for a company advertising hot-dogs, and it is driven to events around the country. It has a hot-dog shaped dashboard and its sun roof is called a 'bun roof'!

Weinermobiles have been touring the USA since 1952. They are so well known that they are even in transport museums.

GOOD MOOD MISSION

Oscar Mayer

Art Station

Here are some ideas for getting creative and designing your own world!

- Design your own boat. Label its special features and give it a name. Where would you sail your boat – on lakes, rivers or the ocean?

- Design a crazy kind of car, like the cars on pages 28 and 29. Label the features of your invention.

- Design some art to go on the side of a bus or a truck. It could be a picture or it could include some words.

- Draw a carnival float that you would like to build for a parade. What is the parade celebrating?

Glossary

Andalucian from Andalucia, a part of southern Spain

amphibious something that can travel on land and in water

blimp a name for an airship, a floating balloon vehicle

Buddhist someone who believes in the religion of Buddhism

cable car a passenger carriage that hangs from cables

chairlift a chair pulled up and down a slope on cables

customise change to make something look different

gondola a rowing boat used in Venice, Italy, or the passenger cabin of a blimp (airship)

harness leather straps fitted on a horse or donkey to help it pull a cart or carry loads

Mennonites a group of people who believes in a particular kind of Christianity

novice beginner

quad bike a motorbike with four large wheels

trishaw a bicycle taxi with a seat for a passenger on the side

vintage a design from the past

wetland a region which is swampy and criss-crossed by streams

Further Information

Websites

**http://www.roughguides.com/article/
10-unusual-types-of-transport/**
Ten unusual kinds of transport from
around the world.

**http://www.sciencekids.co.nz/
sciencefacts/vehicles.html**
Fun facts about the science of different
types of transport.

**http://villageofjoy.com/50-weird-and-
crazy-cars/**
See 50 of the strangest cars from
around the world.

Further Reading

Mapping A Country series
Jen Green (Wayland, 2015)

My Holiday in Italy
Jane Bingham (Wayland, 2014)

Your Local Area: Transport
Ruth Thomson (Wayland 2013)

Index